SURGICAL *Wing*

SURGICAL

Wing

KRISTIN ROBERTSON

ALICE JAMES BOOKS
FARMINGTON, MAINE

10 9 8 7 6 5 4 3 2 1

Alice James Books are published by Alice James Poetry Cooperative, Inc., an affiliate of the University of Maine at Farmington.

Alice James Books
114 Prescott Street
Farmington, ME 04938
www.alicejamesbooks.org

Library of Congress Cataloging-in-Publication Data

Names: Robertson, Kristin, 1975- author.
Title: Surgical wing / Kristin Robertson.
Description: Farmington, ME : Alice James Books, 2017.
Identifiers: LCCN 2016046099 (print) | LCCN 2017002490 (ebook) | ISBN
    9781938584343 (paperback) | ISBN 9781938584442 (eBook)
Subjects: | BISAC: POETRY / American / General.
Classification: LCC PS3618.O316975 A6 2017 (print) | LCC PS3618.O316975
    (ebook) | DDC 811/.6--dc23
LC record available at https://lccn.loc.gov/2016046099

Alice James Books gratefully acknowledges support from individual donors, private foundations, the University of Maine at Farmington, the National Endowment for the Arts, and the Amazon Literary Partnership.

Cover art: "Black Crow" by Michael Creese

Contents

Clinical Trial: Human with Wings: Patient-Reported Outcome, Day 46   3

White Birds   4

Birdwatchers   5

Rules of Surgery   6

Clinical Trial: Human with Wings: Patient-Reported Outcome, Day 7   17

Loon   18

Audubon Ate His Birds   20

Light, Lamb, Follower   22

Lionfish   23

Nagoya   25

Ostrichland   27

Blue Herons   29

Leaving Coins on the Mouths of Cadavers at Emory Hospital, a Defense   31

Alaskan Charter   33

Aubade   35

Nampa-Sha   37

Killing the Geese   38

Hyoid Bone   39

While You Were Out   40

Clinical Trial: Human with Wings: Patient-Reported Outcome, Day 203   43

Moon Elegy   44
Scar   46
Incidental Finding   47
Retiring the Human Name   48
Emergency Rooms during Thunderstorms   50
Letter to Tippi Hedren   51

∂ℐ⌢

Clinical Trial: Human with Wings: Patient-Reported Outcome, Day 91   55

Bonfire   56
Crane Wife   58
Haint Ceilings   60
The Miracle Strip   62
Driving to My Friend's House to Assist Her Suicide   64
Red-Winged Blackbirds   66
Barnyard Door   67
Hiking to Le Cimetière Marin   69
Abecedarian of the Death Moment   70
Swan Song   75

∂ℐ⌢

Clinical Trial: Human with Wings: Patient-Reported Outcome, Day 271   79

How to Transform Your Arm into a Wing   80
You're about to Fold a Paper Airplane   81
Wing   82
Will Humans Ever Have Wings?   83

Acknowledgments

Many thanks to the editors of the publications in which some of these poems first appeared, sometimes in different versions:

Alaska Quarterly Review: "Swan Song"

Bellevue Literary Review: "The Rules of Surgery" and "Scar"

Cimarron Review: "Nagoya"

Construction: "Crane Wife," "Letter to Tippi Hedren," and "Light, Lamb, Follower"

Copper Nickel: "Audubon Ate His Birds"

Crab Orchard Review: "Lionfish" and *"Nampa-Sha"*

Diode Poetry Journal: "Birdwatchers"

The Greensboro Review: "Alaskan Charter"

The Gettysburg Review: "Clinical Trial: Human with Wings"

Harvard Review: "Haint Ceilings"

Indiana Review: "Abecedarian of the Death Moment"

The Journal: "Driving to My Friend's House to Assist Her Suicide" and "Barnyard Door"

The Los Angeles Review: "You're about to Fold a Paper Airplane"

Mid-American Review: "Loon"

Passages North: "Bonfire"

Prairie Schooner: "Hiking to Le Cimetière Marin"

RHINO: "Hyoid Bone"

Smartish Pace: "Incidental Finding"

Spoon River Poetry Review: "White Birds"

storySouth: "Aubade" and "Retiring the Human Name"

Sycamore Review: "Blue Herons," "Leaving Coins on the Mouths of Cadavers at Emory Hospital, a Defense," and "Moon Elegy"

Third Coast: "Ostrichland"

TriQuarterly: "The Miracle Strip"

Willow Springs: "Red-Winged Blackbirds"
Yemassee: "While You Were Out"

"Bonfire" also appeared in *The Southern Poetry Anthology, Volume VI: Tennessee.*

"Audubon Ate His Birds" and "Ostrichland" were also published on *Verse Daily.*

Thank you to David Bottoms, Beth Gylys, Marilyn Kallet, Josh Russell, and Christine Swint.

Much gratitude to Carey Salerno, Alyssa Neptune, Julia Bouwsma, and Michael Broek.

Thank you to the Sewanee Writers' Conference and the Community of Writers at Squaw Valley.

Thank you to my dad, Bill Robertson, and my family for supporting me.

In memory of Jim Morgan.

Special thanks to Sean, Heron, and Summer.

To my mom, Lynn Robertson, this book is for you.

There shall be wings!
—LEONARDO DA VINCI

ONE

Clinical Trial: Human with Wings

Human wings will be here. Mark my words.
—Dr. Joe Rosen, Plastic Surgeon

Patient-Reported Outcome

Day 46

I find myself empathizing with bats,
supposing dragons aren't mythical. Not since
my relevé atop the neighbors' bonfire—
Are these ashes?   Am I rising in flames?—
have I been invited back. I've turned manic.
I've turned manticore. If I belong to anything
anymore, it's the sky, which isn't at all like paradise
if you look at it from eye level. If I were to jump
from a silo or wind turbine, Flyoverland
would hold a candlelight vigil. They can't see
I'm an unearthly being. Closest relative? Lightning.
The hospital asked for an alias, so I researched
angelology: *How art thou cut down to the ground.*
Morning star. Light-bringer. Preparing to fall.

White Birds

After the veteran next to me dies,
the intercom's xylophone requiem signals

night-shift nurses to tape a slapdash white bird,
traced and cut from copy paper, onto our tempered glass.

I watch this pale phoenix ignite its nest
and itself and be reborn whole.

This milk-white raven brings the moon,
fresh water, and fire to the world—

its ivory bill a dead ringer for that extinct woodpecker,
the one they all heard but no one saw.

The next morning, the armored radiologist
lifts my film to the light, circles the white space

below my heart where my insides had been,
and says it looks almost like wings.

Birdwatchers

My two surgeons climbed trees,
        trudged millponds in Arkansas

for the white-billed woodpecker,
        that lonely myth. And on Monday

they gathered their Sunday finds
        and their life birds—

elusive warbler, scarlet tanager—
        over the operating table.

They barnstormed my body
        with talk of crows and ravens,

repeating *Corvidae* in the cornfields,
        Corvidae with the prism-tinted wings,

while they cradled organs they removed
        like baby birds fallen from a nest.

I slept to murders and unkindnesses,
        to the lull of *Corvidae*—

That's *-dee*, not *-day*.   Or *-die*.

Rules of Surgery

—Recited by surgical interns at a nurses' station

Rule 1: Eat When You Can

With the pad of my finger I collect crumb
after crumb like a hopeful, disappearing braille.

Every morning for weeks after my surgery,
I drive halfway to work and then turn around,

head home to press my palms onto the oven, still warm
from toast, just to confirm I have been there.

Birds imprison themselves inside butterfly conservatories,
and we think it's for watermelon and water. But what if

it's for the mirrors—the ones visitors use to check their shirts
for monarchs attracted to nectar-colored stripes?

How else can a bird measure its neon wingspan, see itself
swoop from branch to wrist to a porcelain fruit plate

wild with butterfly wings blinking snake eyes?
They live their lives trapped just to prove,

again and again, they're flying.

Rule 2: Touch the Patient

We called it the tomato dance, summers so warm
we could hear them grow as we lay nightly in the grass—

hiss-swish of vine winding the wooden stakes,
the mammillary thump when the wind picked up.

The Vietnamese gardener at the end of our street
magic-markered grins onto his pie-tin-faced scarecrows

and whip-slung rottens into the woods. We begged him
to try the circle changeup, the knuckle curve.

One afternoon our truck slow-rolled to the stop sign,
and the gardener, wearing his silk-tied paddy hat,

approached the window and lazed his elbow inside.
Our neighbor's dad patted the gardener's coppery arm,

and with a synchronous, nearly undetectable reach,
eased the baseball bat from under our feet.

Rule 3: Sleep When You Can

Home from the hospital
and barely to a lawn chair,

I count starlings. It's easy
to prove you're alive

in daylight and to find
the will to stay that way:

twenty-eight, so far,
on the side of breathe

and keep breathing.
What's harder

is just after nightfall
when the last birds

cannot be counted, before
surgical staples give in

and glint like moon
ripples on a lake,

before toolsheds emit
their nightlong chirps,

invite the first tally
of awakening bats.

Rule 4: Red and Blue Things Bleed

A year after our divorce,
my ex-husband calls from a roadside.

Honest-to-God blue, how he describes
the dying truck driver's mouth.

We hadn't been dating long
when he found me fainted in the shower.

His red towel through the window—
the ambulance's beating heart.

Now, phone shimmed under his ear,
he listens to me breathe

as he waves down cars with a clipboard
like his one good wing.

Rule 5: All Bleeding Stops Eventually

Wound slow to heal,
I meander fretwork

into snowy streets
up to an estate sale.

A basement of medical
paraphernalia—

ebony-handled
decapitation hooks,

phrenology busts,
all the fringe phenomena.

I survey fleam blades
from fish teeth, spring-

loaded scarificators.
At the bloodletting table

I rest an elbow
in the shark-tooth chip

of a saucer, ringed like
a cut tree. Oh, my honey-

stained beauty, what
I'm going to do with you.

Rule 6: Don't Fuck with the Pancreas

Dance around it, new surgeons, like the delicate
liver or ovary of the Japanese fugu:

My lover ate seven courses of the deadly blowfish
one summer night—sashimi, roe, salad once

the spikes were out. With no known antidote,
the first symptom's a tingling in its victim's mouth,

an intoxicating numbness. Prepared live,
scalpeled thin with special knives and petaled

into a chrysanthemum, the funeral flower on a plate,
these puffer fish secrete their own apocrypha,

which, young anglers, will become your pillow talk:
taped mouths scream on the slab, skin winces

at the first slice. But you'll also learn some truths:
once removed the poison parts are locked

inside a metal box, scraped into a barrel
at the fish market, and burned. And the bodies

of the blowfish? They're preserved into lanterns
lighting the sidewalks. They'll follow you home.

TWO

Clinical Trial: Human with Wings

Patient-Reported Outcome

Day 7

What's it like? Not what you think.
It isn't a saturnalia of air and sky-scraped
thrills. Often it's blistering roof shingles.
Reported sightings: *Some kind of Mothman*
at the Quick Trip. The Angel of Death
on my satellite dish. Sidestepping spotlights.
And worse: Today I saw the missing girl.
Her body in a junkyard. That hushed acreage.
Half underneath an abandoned van,
in a nest of barbed wire. From here
I could have watched her lie in hammocks
like the rest of us and waste her beautiful life.
Before she was taken or lured, the girl
ate slices of melon. In a sprinkler. Eyes closed.

Loon

The morning our art teacher claimed her soul
had flown inside her open window the night before—

brushed over her body like a curtain's gauzy hem
and back out—we called her a loon.

From then on we'd cluck and caw, and with our fingers
swirl imaginary rings around our heads

to mimic whatever astral plane she had come from.
Out of the kiln in the back of her auto shop-turned-art room,

we lifted our crackle-glazed waterbirds or—having forgotten
to hollow out the bodies—handfuls of crumbled wings.

We settled into our desks, scattered like floating driftwood,
and again etched feathers into clay with X-Acto knives.

For weeks we hatched for her the better part
of a V formation from that cooling pentagonal egg.

And when we lit a nest of newsprint under her chair,
she fanned her blouse and climbed out the window.

We listened then for her unmistakable wail—
lady lost and soul-searching somewhere downriver.

Audubon Ate His Birds

He gassed them in his closet, and then he pinned
        their wings, feathers splayed like *pick a card*,

any card. He posed them in plastic trees,
        and after his brush had cadmiumed the throat

of the hummingbird, whitewashed
        the spoonbill, he roasted and swallowed

the loves of his life. Like that boy from school—
        walking his first date to the Golden Gallon,

he tied her wrists together with his sweat shirt string
        when she skipped ahead and tried to run,

or the next one he locked in his basement, singing to her
        Percy Sledge, singing, *Hold on to your*

precious love. In a tight-lidded mason jar,
        in a Dixie Cup with a palm over it—

didn't the neighborhood kids smother fireflies
        one at a time, dying like a turned-down oil lamp?

The Duke curtained his first wife, too soon made glad,
      and once a farmwoman, madly in love

with a farmer, dropped the rope tied to his waist
      as he groped through a blizzard

to check the horses. Before her boot caught
      the braid's frayed tip, she imagined him

captured forever inside that barn, pitchforking
      for her any rabid bat, any frenzied sparrow.

Light, Lamb, Follower

My new love offered to write my name—
a single kanji character—

the brush cigared in his teeth
between drafts.

And now I can't remember
what they meant,

those brushstrokes,
night-ink comets and comet tails.

But at midnight, my three sisters
already pinned to his walls,

he dashed off my mother:
Lynn in Japanese means

grove of trees—

and I stood inside it
catching lemons,

bushels and bushels of them,
falling, falling.

Lionfish

After sex I say we need a safe word—
not for rope burns or blindfolds—

but for when he wants to kill himself
and knows, this time, he can pull it off.

He says he's never seen a *lionfish*.
I remember before my cousin's wedding,

as a hurricane backhanded the Alabama coast,
my aunt nestled favors for the reception,

hand-molded, white chocolate seashells,
into coolers of ice in her candlelit kitchen.

From the doorway, my uncle whispered
their saltwater aquarium was starting to die:

five days unfiltered, starfish floating,
algae greening the glass like a rapid frost.

To keep the survivors safe, my aunt dipped
her net into the tank, scooped tang, damsels,

triggerfish, before cornering the poisonous,
feathery predator lurking behind juts of coral.

As she lifted the fish and swiveled
toward the waiting plastic bowl, it slipped

the fragile mesh and flailed to the carpet.
In the second it took her bare hand to reach

for its striped quills, maybe she weighed
its gulping air against the sting, maybe

she saw herself crying on her kitchen floor,
hovering over the cooler, gazing down

at a seashell, like the goddess of love.

Nagoya

My love wrote a poem: the slice
of a woman's chin slips

below an umbrella—
how he aches for its lowering.

A glimpse of her fair skin
to his rainy afternoon?

White-naped crane
to the birdwatcher: no small thing.

I never strolled those curled-wing castles
or warmed on my tongue melon bread

she had tucked inside her purse
from that morning's *panya*.

I wasn't on that sidewalk—

But on this one, I still whisper,
Am I the umbrella?

because we are in love
and maybe he'll answer:

It's your crescent of chin,
your rain-run parasol.

When he says, *No—*
That's not the part of me you own—

I trace my jaw, white as rice powder,
eclipsed by nothing.

Ostrichland

Before I went full-on, pinioned-wing crazy,
        you whisked me on a wine tour, pulled off

the route so I could empty our ashtray change
        onto the counter in front of a lady gripping

a sword-long quill in one hand and cradling an egg
        the size of a toddler's head in the other.

A dollar bought the two of us dustpans of pellets
        the birds bounced with their beaks like jacks.

I swayed toward the chicken wire and *We Bite* signs,
        and you kept your distance, as if to refocus

the whole morning: my aebleskiver tantrum
        at the restaurant in Solvang, one shattered

French press, and this, humming for the emus,
        amber-eyed and weaving their necks

like charmed cobras at my palmsful of feed.
        You'd overheard a myth about the hens:

they incubate their eggs by staring at them.
    I said I wanted to see for myself, so as we left

you bought one, nested it in the cup holder.
    And I watched until it eclipsed the sun and burst

into a hatchling, eating floorboard bottle caps
    and spark plugs and burrowing its head in my lap,

hoping if it could not see, it could not be seen.

Blue Herons

Somewhere outside Mobile,
my cousin perches on a BP bathroom sink.

Her headaches are getting worse,
so we're waiting this one out.

Shadowing *freshwater* onto her brow bone,
she says she'll work at a makeup counter

and rescue seabirds on weekends.
She freed a heron last summer.

Tangled, the fishing line cut diamonds
into its breast. I want to tell her

how my lover studies knots, slips and shanks,
and uses my body to practice, leaves me

sometimes when the tea water boils,
when the neighbor knocks to borrow

his miter saw. I wait with welts like latticework.
My cousin shows me how she'll scrub

an oil-slicked bird, her hands working
the invisible down, prying open its mouth.

When he pours water over my wrists,
roped too tight to the bedposts, he coaches

my fingers awake—*Pink up, pink up*—
and he high-fives them when they do.

I'm driving her to Florida to stay with friends,
to wander the shorelines for the caught

and the flightless. As I cradle her sick head
under the faucet like one of her shorebirds,

I promise next she'll paint me with that fresh
water. I press to my eyelids her blue fingertips.

Leaving Coins on the Mouths of Cadavers at Emory Hospital, a Defense

At doctor camp, the teenagers wire up their lungs
and trigger monitor beeps by holding their breath.

All summer I chaperone, carrying the old coin purse
you shipped from Alaska, cracked leather packed

with unspent change and a quarter-sized bird
carved from caribou bone. Without nightfall,

you can't miss me. Your fear earmarked for bears,
for the haunted lakes. While you drift in icy breakup,

I eavesdrop on my students telling ghost stories—
A headless woman rocks in a chair in a patient room.

When I ask if they've ever seen a decapitated body,
Jamie nods: he and his dad on the Ohio, bass fishing,

pawing their tangled net, and Mary something,
the missing girl, the one from the news—

Her calves were like the blue catfish we threw back.
We sit with the med school cadavers, plastic-veiled,

these overcast islands, and I can't help but think
of you, standing in a flat-bottomed hull

with your lantern and your oar like a boatman
who might return home to ferry souls for a fee—

Alaskan Charter

Fishing the Kachemak takes
more than a hook in a mouth.

When the first catch, weighing
twice a grown man, fights back,

the gang of local fishermen
circle up to stop the thrashing.

After a club thunk to the head,
gaff to the side, the five men resort

to a curb stomp, a filleting knife
to the gill, then someone's .410.

With bloodied shins, you wait
your turn. And then the young fish

they assign you suddenly squirms
in your hands like a newborn

from the womb, slick and risen
and held. You brace yourself

over the gunwale before the fishermen
form a crescent around you,

your back to the warm constant
of the gold sun. They hand you a club

and say, *Don't be a cunt.*
With a fifth strike, the spinal cord

snaps, slips through your fist
like the string of a wind-swiped kite—

and it'll be years before you know,
dipped in black waders, you were

half in your dark grave already.

Aubade

Rats scribble behind sheetrock,
this farmhouse their only sanctuary.

They jot notes in the margins of our bedroom
where once I told you I made rent

three summers working as the Snake Lady
at a county fair. At midnight, I'd rise from my pit

and buy all the vendors' forsaken cotton candy
with dollars children whirligigged down

onto my scales, writhing with the forged magic
of the merfolk, centaurs, and harpies.

Clutching spun sugar bouquets, I'd kiss
the petting zoo goats and lambs funneled

toward their troughs and pine straw,
and zigzag my entrance ramp. I'd vanish

into my trailer with the curtained window.
Somehow, after each show, I'd uncoil

into a warm-blooded woman again.
In the attic, the rats tear hunks of insulation

into pink cumulous, a whole sky I'll gather
by armfuls and climb back down into this life.

Nampa-Sha

Before her husband awoke in my bed
that first morning in my last house,

the one with the lure of mulberry trees,
I shot seventy-eight frames:

the cardinal's breast flaming through branches,
aperture widened to blur all of February.

I tiptoed back to bed, and beside him
I held the camera under my nightgown

to my bare chest, the bird's scarlet pinprick
saved inside white sky   after white sky

after white sky. And then I raised
the warm lens above my head and shot

that happy girl, tumbled her into that white
space, before the next year or the world

falling apart, the girl frozen, but reaching
for something radiant and at arm's length.

Killing the Geese

You ended the affair on the same day
they killed the geese for loving fresh mown grass

so reminiscent of their prairie homes.
A campus built on wetlands. Man-made ponds,

those edges prime for hiding sink-size nests.
They fed on popcorn all winter term; their shit

was weighed in pounds. Their periscoping necks
steadfast on streets despite the hunting dogs

and constant mist machines that mimicked fog.
And even when the men, USDA,

addled their eggs with buckets of corn oil,
deprived their embryos of air, we found

the matted furrows leading to the shore
where hens had rolled their eggs to rinse them clean.

Hyoid Bone

Lonely versus *lonesome*,
seeking a companion or pitifully forlorn,

distinguished at the point of ossification,
which is adolescence, when the human body's

only bone not connected to another
hardens at the neck's midline.

Evolved from the fish, its gill arches,
this horseshoe behind the tongue helps us

speak when it itself has no one to listen—
omega fallen behind the pack, wolf pup

vulnerable to bears. Last night they found
the runaway, her young body

in a split-leather back seat, miles from
the lightning flash of her truck stop.

The only way to fracture the body's hyoid,
forsaken upsilon, is to strangle it.

While You Were Out

I didn't answer the phone when you called,
just let it ring like a child practicing phonetics,

there and
this way

and *thə*
and *thē*.

I didn't make lists of why
you needed me after all this time,

no reasons for your sudden wanting.
Maybe you got down to the lake again,

and it was high from rain. You thought of me—
bent backward into a bridge,

my hands sunk into the mud
at the edge of the water,

your hands lifting my waist
for an ocean liner to pass under us.

THREE

Clinical Trial: Human with Wings

Patient-Reported Outcome

Day 203

I keep thinking about the instant Voyager 1
crossed into interstellar space. On board,
its Golden Record, the story of our world
to other spacefarers. In fifty-five languages:
Wishing you a peaceful future from the earthlings.
I would have said: rats live on no evil star.
When I try to sleep, I hear it, that murmur.
Mechanical moan of lonesomeness.
The sound of a shadow, of a passing
cloud. And whenever I dream, I tie an album
to my chest with string. In a few years,
the first Voyager will stop returning calls.
Forever flying with only the taped litanies
of surf: *Tonight you're simply too far away.*

Moon Elegy

We can't write about the moon anymore,
even as we stand here holding spatulas,

our children in the middle of the street,
lured from their homes like the tide.

Tonight we're so close to those craters
we almost smell the gunpowder snow.

On the front lawn of her foreclosed house,
a neighbor sets the dining room table.

But we can't call it a chandelier in the sky,
even for her. And we can't remember

the bright surgical lamp, nurses above us
exhaling, *You almost didn't wake up.*

When the neighbor rises from her chair
to retie her white bathrobe, we can't imagine

Artemis and ask if she'll take us with her.
If we search the dictionary for *Lunar Perigee*,

the closest moon ever to the Earth, we'll find it
cast after *Pedigree* and *Peregrine*—

stay and feed the dog, or fly away?

Scar

First night home from the hospital, I start a list
of what we leave covered, like old Tupperware

behind the milk, or tombs. In sixth grade I built
a viewing box for a solar eclipse, caught the black sun,

and never again lifted the lid. I left it
on the floor of my closet until the cat crawled in

and died. My mother never looked,
buried it all—the cat, the sun—in our backyard.

Some ancient ruins rest cordoned forever,
no sweaty palms against hieroglyphs

or breathy fumblings of a hermetic prayer.
I lie here in the dark, my stapled abdomen

like a mouth with my hand over it. And in the kitchen,
my lover changes the burned-out fridge bulb

after groping blind for cold noodles. In front of the open
door, he's eating from the carton and letting out the light.

Incidental Finding

Over five years my surgical scar has cooled
to a pale fault line, the slow tectonics of healing,

but this morning the doctor again unscrolls an x-ray,
points to a ghostlike wisp, and repeats the word *mass*,

scarier even than the word *shark* or the word *missing*.
But not scarier than *malignant*, from *malign*, to speak evil of.

I hear it in the hiss through aspens as I wait for pathology,
barefoot on a balcony in a hospital gown and overcoat.

Siblings of ill children skate to the lake's bull's-eye
and lie on their stomachs with their ears pressed to the ice.

They listen for the groans and bone-cracks of a body
of water frozen to its core. And with the weight of pike fishers

and ptarmigans, a capsized canoe, and the kids' warm breaths
forecasting an inevitable spring, the ice refuses, even then, to break.

Retiring the Human Name

What I want to do in my Adirondack
next to a one-legged man

on the porch of the last seafood place
slinging swai po' boys and bottled beer

before the hurricane evacuation
is ask how he lost it.

I'd hear about his crab trap
sprung at the bay shore, his slip,

his knee scrape and bruise—
first maybe the size of a sea flea,

growing to a sea horse brood pouch,
and by dusk, big as a seafloor tar ball

tumbling toward him in the night,
red streaks eeled up his thigh.

The doctor in the ER told him:
I'll give it to you straight.

What I do is watch the local women
who'll stay through the storm,

their hair whipping around them
as if under the water already.

I help secure a skirt, chase a sun hat, as the wind—
oh, the wind—as the man with one leg

explains, *Ivan means John in Russian*,
as he catches a woman's gold earring

midair, as it flashes over his head like a beacon.
So many Ivans, he says, *the great and the terrible*.

Emergency Rooms during Thunderstorms

Condors step into pie slice after pie slice
        of these revolving doors. Here so long

we feel almost extinct. Homeless men
        scoop up passenger pigeons like newborns

or harvested hearts. When the lights flicker,
        only febrile children can comfort the siege

of night herons rejected from lighthouses
        full of seabirds categorized Least Concern.

Species of fernbirds and white-eyes nestle
        inside our raincoats next to chest pains.

Dodos perch on broken fibulas. OD'ing teens
        inhale Carolina parakeets to sing in their lungs.

All of us, lost in the wild. The spectacled
        cormorants, the accidents with glass.

Letter to Tippi Hedren

Remember after Hitch said, *Enough pretending*,
let's put real birds in, how you went on with your life,

strolled past two crows pecking dunes of cornmeal
off a muffin pan in the street. You didn't gauge

their caws too close to a conversation or conspiracy.
All this time I've looked to you to confirm

the numbers of terns or skimmers, the laughing gulls,
low hoverers ever closer to the hand's stale baguette.

Please don't admit now that you can't be sure.
When geese stop traffic, loosed upon the world

on my morning commute, or when I count forty-seven
hummingbirds at the feeder, keep the truth to yourself.

Allow me my awe, my sweet joy when a hawk lands
on the hood of a car, graceful and intended as a leaf.

FOUR

Clinical Trial: Human with Wings

Patient-Reported Outcome

Day 91

The condemned men must find me
the unlikeliest of angels, sitting next to them
after their last meal of fried chicken
and sweet peas. Or over-easy eggs
and toast. A single olive with the pit
still inside. It's where I spend most of my time,
comforting murderers. Everyone wants
to feel of use. After the chaplains and mothers
have gone, I try to sort the prisoners'
earliest memories, like petals into cupped hands.
Soon the guards are Bradford pears.
And caged out, I pray before their walk
to the death chamber, pray the cold row
blooms into an esplanade of cherry trees.

Bonfire

This could be what dying feels like,
here, at dusk, on Dockweiler State Beach,

so close to the blaze I could half-pivot
the sand and trust-fall in toward someone shouting,

Cool hat! or *How about some frisbee?* from the other side.
Within these busted pallets and flames

my dead uncle practices karate kicks,
same leg swift-striking the air like a snake's tongue,

then tai chi, white crane spreading its wings, his arms
open wide, like Zoroaster, summoning this fire

for me. Farther down shore, with smoke in my sleeves,
I stall, play Jenga with firewood. I sip from a red cup.

Under the last of the sun, pelicans barrel
toward the widening pupil of glittering ocean.

I hear my mother, back in Tennessee, at the screen door:
Play in the sandbox after dinner until you no longer

see your own hand in front of your face.
Then you must come in.

Crane Wife

After my mother tosses a sleeping kitten into the dryer
with a basketful of my father's laundry,

she bows over the kitchen sink for hours,
her long hair hanging like water frozen from a faucet.

She drowns his shirts, twists the bleached sleeves
between her raw fists, like the myth

of the crane wife curling over a loom, weaving
white bolts for her poor husband to sell.

When he discovered her, plucking her own feathers
to spin into cloth, she flew away—

Always we tried to wrangle the newborn kittens,
but with paraffin eyes they wandered under sofas

or woodpiles, and sometimes we found them dead
and piecemeal, the mother cat leaving only

what she couldn't swallow. At nightfall,
resisting our pleas for red apples she'd be forced

to core and portion with a knife, my mother piles
the still pink-tinged shirts onto the front lawn.

As headlights flood the driveway, she slips her arms
inside shirttails, an origami wingspan

answering wind, answering the whooping calls.

Haint Ceilings

The Gullah culture of the Lowcountry believes that spirits, known as "haints," can't cross water. Using light blue paint to symbolize water, the Gullah people applied the shade to porch ceilings and doors preventing evil spirits from entering.
——*Southern Living*

Your dead neighbor straddles your windowsill,
duct-taping her cardboard wings to her bathrobe,

determined to fly and then flying, this time,
like a swallow skimming your pool for a drink.

Someone's grandmother cusses her cold cream
halfway up your staircase, and you glimpse

her painted-on stocking seams, her victory rolls,
a flicker of white gloves she wore only to the bank.

A stewardess leans against your repurposed pie safe,
tells you she worked three ships before they sank,

including *Titanic*, tells you her name's Violet Jessop.
She rinses three scalloped aprons in your farm sink.

But you're really only painting your porch ceiling
to keep out two college students, a boy and a girl,

who were raped and tortured and left to die
the first year you taught writing. They're always

on your front lawn, asking to hand in their love poems
from the day they were buried, that missed class.

The Miracle Strip

Panama City Beach, Florida

After long naps, the children on beach vacation
sip Dr. Chek and wonder why they're eating

hot dogs for breakfast. The black cherry cola
stains their mouths awestruck. Somewhere

beyond their five-deep hammock, a roller coaster
moans like a sad whale. They venture out

from under the streetlight toward the waterfront
amusement park, The Miracle Strip.

Their cutoffs' ripped hems like *cilia, flagella*—
words they've yet to learn—tremble against the thigh.

Their young bodies lured by Tilt-A-Whirl strobes
and the radio stah uh ah uh ah uh ah ar.

They must be just this tall, and they are.
And then they hesitate at the entrance. A blink.

A skip in the heart. Before the line to wander up
the devil's tongue and be strapped in,

before the funhousing, the just-one-more-ride-ing,
in this middle distance they feed their gum to sea gulls.

They thumb their soft wrists before snapping tight
wristbands red as red never found in nature.

Driving to My Friend's House to Assist Her Suicide

The two of us have a plan and a mixtape
from fifth grade, the year we hid marbles

under our tongues. Mine, clear and galaxy-centered.
Hers, always like a cloud neither of us could

see through. She's terminal as waterfalls or runaway
trains and doesn't live in Oregon, a death

with dignity state, snowy with aspens, ticker tape
petals everywhere: It's all over. Celebrate now.

So I'm to push play and scoop her pills
into souvenir teaspoons. She says we can't touch—

like two birds perched on this live wire.
They would arrest me, she says, ask how I did it.

Maybe they'd ask if I rested her sandpiper neck
in my palm, her serif spine over my knee.

Ask me if I looked at her as a herd looks
back at the bitten, the flailing, the already gone.

Ask me if I sang along with "A Whiter
Shade of Pale," and somewhere in the middle,

after *turned cartwheels* and before *her face at first
just ghostly*, if I hid under her tongue a cluster of stars.

Red-Winged Blackbirds

New Year's Day

Your bodies lie like burning holes on lawns,
on sidewalks, where housewives clutch their throats

and watch their children spread your wings. What dawn
is this? Firemen palm hunks of fallen soot

and nestle you into pails. You fail to give
a reason: chimneys, updraft, lightning,

the revelers with sparks and blasts? Forgive
our midnight, our dark bricks, our frightening

love calls, our need to touch your shoulder's red
roulette chip and compare your flock, your fate,

to Little Rock fish kills, the bluegill dead.
All year our hand will hold your constant weight:

a clump of seaweed, a fist of tangled hair,
our kicked-up divot, iris bulb, a pear.

Barnyard Door

My cousin's mare trips
headfirst onto a tiny rock,

some chthonic arrowhead,
and I stand at a barnyard door.

Barnyard door,

the phrase second-language third graders
voted prettiest English.

When drug dogs surrounded
my coke-dealing boyfriend's house,

I balled up in the shower stall
and whispered my strange hosanna,

Barnyard door. Barnyard door,

when doctors sighed at scans of
my sunburst spleen, my meteoric ovary.

Now, the gate unlatched for her long
walk toward the mare's

final breaths, the definition of mist,
I chant those words like a canticle—

Barnyard door—

and, this time, weathered wood,
the laying on of hands.

Hiking to Le Cimetière Marin

Sick as a dog in Sète, I don't tell Sonja
who's hell-bent on seeing Valéry's grave.

I snap in half these fishing-town gimcracks,
souvenir shell rings and whistlers, objets d'art

for our winding footpath, anything to distract
myself from pain sharp as sea change.

Ahead she traces scars on headstones, dried funeral
rosebuds like pill cups flush with salt spray.

At these cliffs, where scores of stone Marys
overlook the Mediterranean, surrender feels right—

give up your dove, your angel, whatever lightness
helped you get here. Watch your white wings turn to sails.

Abecedarian of the Death Moment

Alien abductees, all the mysteries, the unexplained, wait on you
under awnings as if for tables at a Michelin-starred restaurant.

~

Bermuda triangle ships, vulturous in their circling, all accounted for,
ferry you into a pearl harbor undrowned and oh so visible.

~

Clairaudients press seashells to your ears. *What kind of*
are you are you? Now you know. You hear ducks and playgrounds.

~

Your Doppelgänger replaces all the mirrors with windows
because why not and you'll want to see what happens next.

~

The Exorcised, full of ambrosial air, float by you like zeppelins,
weightless manatees, unendangered and worthy of petting.

~

Feral children huddle on carousels you once loved, gilded tigers
and ostriches and wolves. You find ride tickets up your sleeves.

⁓

Ghosts, back before appetizers, spot their reserved seating
and sell updates for aperitifs: yes, he's feeding your cats.

⁓

Into the Hollow Moon you usher the haunting elephants, culled
from their societies, *remembering remembering* like thunder.

⁓

The Immortals—the Nephites, Merlin, Achilles—ask for
your clothes and bike, your drugstore alchemy, your tendons.

⁓

The Jersey Devil begs for scraps and purrs; under a white
tablecloth it stacks its own illusory bones like kindling.

⁓

Everyone twists Kaikoura lights like balloon animals
to wave over squid boats. Maybe the motherless kids will smile.

⁓

The Loch Ness lets you tether yourself to it. Call the plesiosaur
algae bloom or pinewood. Afterlife takes getting used to.

~

Mermaids rake sea treasure onto your feet, coins and chains.
Consider it hush money. Or rent for real estate beyond the sandbars.

~

Nostradamus, at the head of your table, prophesies islands
of plastic in the gyres. Warns with seismic waves and wildfires.

~

Ouija, a letter banner from here to there, threads *M*, threads *I*,
threads *S* then *S* then *you* and *you*. Threads *perhaps a few others*.

~

Here the Paranormal skydive. Para- means alongside. Parachute
means alongside a fall. Paradise means alongside a wall.

~

Quark stars? Strange but jugglable. The dropped become sparks
in irises, a geode's core. Speedboat paint. The magpie's haul.

~

You visit the Roswell gift shop: wreckage like squares of fudge wrapped in tinfoil, chunks of their planet like the Berlin.

～

You weigh your Soul on a two-pan balance, counterweigh mayfly or snowmelt. Allow for error from the dusty or the magnetic.

～

A Tarot trump, the Hanged Man advises you on letting go:
Be a wolf, a crayfish, a satyr. Be winged, if you want.

～

UFOs, in your palms like pigeons or lanterns, ready themselves for home. Trembling and humming, they ready themselves for light.

～

A Vortex back to your universe, a hippo in your kitchen holding open its mouth for white grapes like galaxies. Stay or go.

～

The Wonderman, the Count of St. Germain, delivers a postcard from his wanderings: resting in a ploughed row of your field.

～

Extraterrestrials gossip next to you, but you skywatch anyway.
The mysteries now? The kite, the bi-wing, the white-throated swift.

~

Yeti face is cupped in your hands like the boy's who stole your wheel-
barrow for joy-wheeling in cul-de-sacs like earth crescents.

~

A Zombie confesses: she lingers inside a body to walk the streets
of this tender world. And to terrorize. One more than the other.

Swan Song

Your body will fight forward-slash forearm cuts.

When you come undone, when you float toward the razor
on the lip of your bathtub, float down

the night-quiet hall like a swan through an inlet,
know your body won't make this easy.

Its coagulants will render cells into syrup.
Skin fibers will interweave like microscopic fingers

playing *here's the church*. Just like your body fights
cherry clear moonshine from a thigh-held mason jar,

siphons it through the liver, into sugar, and gone.
Know your body will squeeze beautiful oxygen

from a barren capillary, feed blood to the most resistant heart.

FIVE

Clinical Trial: Human with Wings

Patient-Reported Outcome

Day 271

Today I bought a gun safe at Sports Authority.
Not a bank vault or fuse box decoy, a clock safe
with bird automaton. I'm waiting for the last
of the cuckoos, the moment when its fulcrum
rests in the dark. I've installed fritted glass,
mastered bird spikes and zero-zero mornings.
I slip fallen feathers into my knife block. Eagle
Scouts teach when to let go of a blade—
only after the receiver says, *I have the knife*.
Leonardo grounded his flying machine made of
pine, lashings, and raw silk. Closed his mirrored
codices of fossils and dissected birds, those soaring
kites. I've decided to *release* means to *hope*.
It means while surrendering, you kiss the ground.

How to Transform Your Arm into a Wing

—After an article published in New Scientist

It can be done. When fusing fingers, leave
the thumb, a free alula (helps to land).

And weld the carpals of the wrist and hand
to model after Archaeopteryx,

first bird. Rework the skin and muscle. Change
the human keratin. Instead of hair,

the thickening of feathers. Four meters
of wingspan are required for human flight.

And then forever give up violin,
a pen, your rings, the button shirt,

to join the wrens and angels. Say, *One could
do worse than fly.* And yet this morning when

my husband went to hold our one-year-old,
before he entered, on her door, he knocked.

You're about to Fold a Paper Airplane

Build evidence of air. Pull the results of your blood test
from the mailbox. Fold in half: you have wings already.

Abnormal? Fold again. You can't see the inner workings
of an aircraft. And when you're folding, you can't study

much else. Book your tumor markers a flight to Bora Bora.
Vector, Victor. Clearance, Clarence. On any scrap of paper

Write, *Carry*. Write, *Heavenward*. Write, *I choose this over you*.
Replace *this*. With *flying*. With *peregrination*. Or write,

I can't fear you another morning. And fold. Exit row pressed
against exit row. Live overlaps die. Fold again to make a fighter jet,

my thunderbird. My blue angel. Whisper, *That's right, Ice
Man. I am dangerous*. Now it's in your hands like a wished-on crane

saving your uncle from a cancer, lifting your sister from a well.
Write inside the crease, the cockpit: *All my fury*. And fold.

Now you can go on and get serious living. Roger, Roger.

Wing

—*After "The Red Poppy" by Louise Glück*

The great thing / is not having / a mind.

I fan the sun, stars, all the flames
        from great and greater distances.

It is true I'm hinged. Diptyched.
        Doppelgängered. But I know

the scrutable peace of the synchronized pair.
        The pitch to another's yaw.

Allow me to speak on behalf of both of us:
        Ancient humans flew, once,

to learn delight. You see traces when
        they wave. When they worship

something. When they toss their babies
        into the sky, that blue unit of measure.

Will Humans Ever Have Wings?

—*From Yahoo Answers*

That will probably NEVER happen.
Evolution produces only what is NECESSARY,

not what is cool. It's possible scientists could mix DNA
with humans and birds and get wings on a human,

but without feathers most likely. But it would be an 8% chance.
You don't want to just go down the angel path.

Make a pair of wings for yourself and measure them.
We'd flop around until we came crashing down to earth.

It takes time for our bodies to realize we need to make a change.
You know those old movies where people put wings

on a car and try to fly it? Never worked, did it?
That's because it takes more than wings. Just look at birds,

especially those we eat. No one knows which way we are going.
You have it backwards, and I am so not surprised.

RECENT TITLES FROM ALICE JAMES BOOKS

The Blessing of Dark Water, Elizabeth Lyons

Reaper, Jill McDonough

Madwoman, Shara McCallum

Contradictions in the Design, Matthew Olzmann

House of Water, Matthew Nienow

World of Made and Unmade, Jane Mead

Driving without a License, Janine Joseph

The Big Book of Exit Strategies, Jamaal May

play dead, francine j. harris

Thief in the Interior, Phillip B. Williams

Second Empire, Richie Hofmann

Drought-Adapted Vine, Donald Revell

Refuge / es, Michael Broek

O'Nights, Cecily Parks

Yearling, Lo Kwa Mei-en

Sand Opera, Philip Metres

Devil, Dear, Mary Ann McFadden

Eros Is More, Juan Antonio González Iglesias, Translated by Curtis Bauer

Mad Honey Symposium, Sally Wen Mao

Split, Cathy Linh Che

Money Money Money | Water Water Water, Jane Mead

Orphan, Jan Heller Levi

Hum, Jamaal May

Viral, Suzanne Parker

We Come Elemental, Tamiko Beyer

Obscenely Yours, Angelo Nikolopoulos

Mezzanines, Matthew Olzmann

Lit from Inside: 40 Years of Poetry from Alice James Books, Edited by Anne Marie Macari and Carey Salerno

Black Crow Dress, Roxane Beth Johnson

Dark Elderberry Branch: Poems of Marina Tsvetaeva,
A Reading by Ilya Kaminsky and Jean Valentine

Alice James Books has been publishing poetry since 1973. The press was founded in Boston, Massachusetts as a cooperative wherein authors performed the day-to-day undertakings of the press. This collaborative element remains viable even today, as authors who publish with the press are also invited to become members of the editorial board and participate in editorial decisions at the press. The editorial board selects manuscripts for publication via the press's annual, national competition, the Alice James Award. Alice James Books seeks to support women writers and was named for Alice James, sister to William and Henry, whose extraordinary gift for writing went unrecognized during her lifetime.

Designed by Pamela A. Consolazio
LITTLE FROG DESIGNS

Printed by McNaughton & Gunn